Warman's

# MATCHBOX ®

## FIELD GUIDE

REGD. U.S. PAT. OFF.  MARCA REGISTRADA

"MATCHBOX" Series

A LESNEY PRODUCT

33

"MATCHBOX" REGD. T.M. G.B. AND ABROAD  MADE IN ENGLAND

Tom Larson

*Values and Identification*

©2006 Krause Publications
Published by

 **krause publications**

*An Imprint of F+W Publications*

**700 East State Street • Iola, WI 54990-0001**
**715-445-2214 • 888-457-2873**

Our toll-free number to place an order or obtain
a free catalog is (800) 258-0929.

Library of Congress Catalog Number: 2005906848
ISBN: 0-89689-300-6

Designed by Kay Sanders
Edited by Karen O'Brien

Printed in China

*To Shelly, Lauren, and Danielle*

# Contents

## How to Use This Book

Matchbox™ cars are presented in numerical order within each of the above chapters. The listing below each photo contains the Matchbox™ number, a description, year of release, and value. The abbreviation "MIMB" stands for Mint-In-Mint-Box and is the highest condition grade issued to a car. It implies that not only is the car in mint condition, so is its box. See p.11 for a further explanation of condition.

# Introduction

Welcome to the hobby of Matchbox™ toys.

Matchbox™ has offered a vast array of toys throughout its 50+ years of history. This guide concentrates on the castings from the "1-75" line of toys. The popular 1-75 line features vehicles in 1:64 scale and are most recognizable to collectors as "Matchbox" cars. Die-cast toy cars about 3" in length are often called "Matchbox" even if they were made by other companies. I will leave it to others to chronicle the Models of Yesteryear, King Size, Convoys, and other lines.

These toys can be broken up into three eras. The first era of models is called "Regular Wheels." Characterized by a thick nail axle with heavy metal or plastic wheels, Regular Wheels were made from 1953 until 1969. These realistic models are finely detailed and required a child's imagination for

motion and play value. Almost exclusively, Regular Wheels were packaged in individual "Matchbox" boxes that featured a picture or drawing of the individual model.

The second era of models is "Lesney Superfast." These toys were necessitated by the 1969 release and rapid popularity of Mattel's Hot Wheels™. Lesney had to convert their slower-moving models to the new "speed" wheels. To compete with the new die-cast upstart, Superfast™ models gradually employed wild colors and big engines similar to those of Hot Wheels™. The Lesney Superfast™ era ended with the bankruptcy of Lesney in 1982. The era of "Made in England" also ended with Lesney. Models were still available in boxes, but the use of blisterpacks became more common in the late 1970s, and the remaining boxes were generic in appearance by the end of the Lesney Superfast™ era.

The third era of Matchbox™ toys is the "Post Lesney 1-75." These are the models made by the other companies that have owned the Matchbox™ name since Lesney was sold and are typically manufactured in countries such as China, Macau, and Thailand. Almost exclusively available in blisterpack form, Matchbox™ packaging ceased to be of great collecting interest during this era.

Collectors pursue each era enthusiastically. With more than 50 years of history, you will never get bored or come to the end of collecting Matchbox™ toys.

This book is a good introduction to Matchbox™ toys as it shows the most readily available models and includes values for each. This should provide collectors with a good sampling of value by era. I will give some collecting tips and resources for further study. Hopefully, this will be a first of a personal library of toy books fueling your collecting interests.

Tom Larson

Thanks to Jake Schultz, Don Hutchinson, Don Windham, and Mark Curtis.

# History

Two school friends, Leslie Smith and Rodney Smith, started Lesney Products. They met again in the English Royal Navy in 1940 and decided they would like to form a company after the war was over. The company was created in 1947 with government surplus die-casting equipment and housed in an old tavern in Edmonton, London. The "Lesney" name was a composite of the two owner's first names. They decided to make pressure die-casting products for industrial use. Lesney was one of several companies making small die-cast pieces in London at the time, and both founders retained their day jobs for many years.

Jack Odell joined Lesney early on and was called upon for his skill in die-casting. He became a key member of the Lesney team.

Because of the English tax system, reduced orders for goods during the last few months of the year made business pretty slow. Many of the die-cast companies made Christmas toys during this slow time. Lesney produced its first toy, the Aveling-Barford Road Roller, and sold to a few local London shops in 1948. This toy was much larger than the later Matchbox™ series of toys. Over the next few years Lesney released a variety of toys including vehicles, animals, and horse drawn wagons.

In 1953, Lesney started the Matchbox™ series by creating smaller versions of some of the early large toys. The first three were a Road Roller™, Dumper, and Cement Mixer. Since Lesney did not want to take on the marketing, packaging, and distribution of their toys they teamed up with the Moko Company to handle distribution. The early boxes read, "A Moko Lesney Toy." Moko received a percentage of the selling price and put their name on all toys they distributed no matter what company manufactured them. Moko owned 50% of the Matchox™ trademark. Around this time Rodney Smith left Lesney and Jack Odell helped manage the company with Leslie Smith.

Lesney bought out Moko in 1958 and fully owned the Matchbox™ series. The boxes were changed to read, "A Lesney Product." Lesney created the Model of Yesteryear™ line in 1956 and Major Pack line in 1958. Lesney quickly expanded to other markets in Europe, Asia, and the U.S.

Fred Bronner became the sole U.S. distributer of Matchbox™ in this period and Lesney bought him out to create Lesney Products (U.S.A.). Bronner became the first president.

The 1960s was a high flying period for Lesney as the King Size models debuted and the company shipped some six million toys per week to nearly every country in the world.

In 1969, Lesney and Matchbox™ faced their biggest challenge yet. Mattel released their immensely popular "Hot Wheels" brand of vehicles and the sales of Matchbox™ models plummeted quickly. Although Matchbox™ models were highly detailed and beautiful models, they did not roll quickly. Their thick axles and heavy plastic wheels made them more of a static model fueled the imagination of a child that rolled them by hand on playsets like "Matchbox City" or in the backyard sandbox with dump truck and contruction vehicles. Mattel's innovative advertising showed their new brightly-painted cars whizzing down the famous orange track doing loops and jumps.

Thankfully for Lesney, their was no patent on this new thin-axle fast-acting wheel design. Matchbox™ quickly adapted and introduced "Superfast" cars by converting the old designs to new fast acting wheels and bright colors. By the end of 1970, almost the entire line up was converted to Superfast™ wheels and track sets were being sold by Matchbox™.

During the 1970s Lesney diversified its offerings to include dolls, and even purchased the AMT model kit company. The late '70s were not kind to Lesney.

There was a nationwide power strike, a worker strike, and a fire at a key facility. This combined with the rising costs of business, further expansion into other businesses, and a downturn in the economy caused Lesney to over-extend itself. On June 11, 1982, Lesney Products was put into receivership.

The toy company was renamed "Matchbox Toys Ltd." and was purchased by David Ych and Universal Toys. The industrial die-casting company still exists as Lesney. Universal toys quickly moved production of most toys to Macau. This greatly reduced the cost of production in England. Universal Toys also branded many of the company's other toys as Matchbox™. Even Pee Wee Herman dolls were marketed under the Matchbox brand. In 1987, Matchbox™ bought the Dinky™ trademark, bringing a second famous English die-cast company to the Universal Toys family.

Universal was purchased by Tyco Toys of Mt. Laurel, New Jersey, in 1992. Tyco™ was a large company known for HO trains, electric racing sets, and radio controlled cars. During this time Tyco™ released a popular line of Matchbox™ die cast toys featuring characters from Sesame Street. Tyco™ also created a strong line of mail-order Models of Yesteryear™ vehicles. These new Models of Yesteryear™ models featured greatly detailed cold cast loads not seen before.

Another parent company was around the corner for the Matchbox™ brand when Mattel, the world's largest toy company, purchased Tyco Toys in 1997. Mattel had previously acquired Corgi Toys, and its addition of Tyco™ meant that Mattel now owned the copyrights to the three largest English makers of die-cast cars. Matchbox™ struggled for turf in Mattel and made some early mistakes. How Wheels™ were certainly the favored brand.

But there is new hope. A new marketing team for Matchbox™ was formed in 2004 and the brand seems to have regained a little of what has histori-cally made it strong. The new team is bringing back realism and quality to our favorite brand. Matchbox™ has a bright future.

# Collecting Tips

**1. Start small.** Collect only what you like! Be yourself and don't follow the crowd. Collectors can get burned out and extremely frustrated trying to collect everything.

Start with a focus. Try to collect all the models from a single year or try to find every one of this year's 1-75 core line. With more than 50 years of history, collecting everything Matchbox™, even in one category, is too big for most collectors and can be overwhelming.

**2. Be patient.** Because there are not many truly rare Matchbox™ models, this week's must-have "rare" new model will be in next year's two-for-a-dollar pile. If you do not have to be the first to have a model, you will be happier and richer. The hobby is rife with people we call "scalpers," who literally vacuum the stores of all new and allegedly hard-to-find models and try to sell them at an inflated price.

This type of post retail sale is the antithesis of Matchbox™ collecting. To counter it, develop friendships with other collectors. Very often, the car you cannot find may be sitting on your friend's desk and you could trade evenly for one not found where you are. Networking remains a vital aspect of the hobby because Matchbox™ maintains its practice of making different models for different global locations. Patience is the virtue of the Matchbox™ collector.

**3. Make friends.** Try to find others who enjoy your hobby. You can meet others on Internet message boards, at local toy shows, or even in the toy aisles. Friends in the hobby can help you find the models you need while adding fun and enthusiasm to the search.

Meet for breakfast with some local collectors and show and tell. I literally have friends throughout the world, some of whom I shall never meet face to face, but they often share their finds with me and I cherish them.

**4. Display and play with your toys.** Find a place to put your models on display. Even with a small space, you can have fun by rotating models in and out of your display.

Run the new model around on your desk or on the floor. Do you remember getting down at the level of your toys and really looking at them? I do! It is no fun to have your models in a box in a closet.

**5. Have a budget.** Decide what you can afford. With the oldest models now over 50 years old and many worth $100+ in Mint-in-Box form, some consideration must be given toward budgeting your hobby dollars. You can build a super collection of older models for $10 or $15 each if you select models without boxes and in lesser condition. Honest playwear on a model is a badge of honor among many collectors and you can build a terrific collection of "used" models for the price of a few truly Mint-in-Box showcase pieces.

**6. Collect the paper.** Matchbox™ produced a lot of ephemera currently desired by collectors. Some collectors have made a hobby completely of collecting the wide variety of Matchbox™ catalogs. A Matchbox™ catalog or poster was released virtually every year since 1957. These catalogs were produced in a variety of languages and sent to nations around the globe.

Dealer-only items are another collecting avenue. Cardboard model displays, Matchbox™ display "spinners," sales posters, dealer catalogs, and even original boxes are quite valuable today because most were tossed away as dealers moved on to the next promotion. There are also lots of magazine advertisements for Matchbox™ that look great framed as part of your display.

One interesting note: The designers of our little toy cars often participate in our yearly conventions, like the MCCH's International Gathering of Friends. They often will sign posters and blisterpacks of the cars they designed.

**7. There is a never-ending supply.** Matchbox™ models have been produced for over 50 years. In the 1960s, Matchbox™ was manufacturing 6 million models a week. If you think a model is priced too high today, just pass on it. There will be another one just around the corner, except for the rarest of the rare models. You may find over years of collecting that you passed on a few good deals, but most of the time your instincts will guide you correctly.

**8. Don't collect for investment.** Toy cars are a luxury and their perceived value is varied and transitory. The old models are worth more today because they were toys and not collector's items when new. The new releases will never be worth big money because there are too many collectors packing them away in unplayed-with condition. Finding a 1950s model that has never been removed from its box is quite rare today, but the same will not be said of 2005 models in 2055 because of the efforts of collectors to preserve mint-in-package examples.

Collect what you like and you will never be disappointed that the value does not greatly exceed what you paid. You will still enjoy the beauty of your collection.

**9. Condition matters!** Learn the "C" code of condition. This is a basic 1-10 condition scale used by many collectors. A model that is C10 is perfect in every way: truly a "mint-in-box" model. Many brand new models are not perfect, so be careful about calling your models C10 or "mint." Many collectors will rate both the box and the model with a "C" condition code. A model with the slightest imperfection will be rated a C9. Many models that you find in garage sales will probably be a condition C6 or C7, which means they are complete, but the wheels have wear and the paint has a good deal of chipping. A model that is a C5 is complete with all parts but really beat up.

### 10. Join a club.

### Matchbox™ Collector's Community Hall (MCCH)

This is probably the best Internet site to share information about Matchbox™. People from all corners of the world participate and network there. This site is run by Mark Curtis, and has active forums for collectors of all brands of die-cast, especially Matchbox™.

Joining and participation is free. Mark can be reached for more information at mark@mboxcommunity.com or at his Web site: http://www.mbox-community.com

### The Matchbox™ International Collectors' Association (MICA)

P.O. Box 120
Deeside, CH5 3HE
United Kingdom
http://www.matchboxclub.com/

MICA is based in the UK but widely read throughout the world. The club publishes a bi-monthly full-color newsletter that is highly regarded. There is good focus on Models of Yesteryear™ and Code 2 models, yet it still covers new 1-75 issues.

### Matchbox™ Forum International

http://www.mbxforum.com/

Matchbox Forum is an international club of Matchbox collectors exchanging information mainly via the Internet.

### Matchbox™ USA

Charles Mack

62 Saw Mill Rd.

Durham, CT 06422

Phone: (860) 349-1655

E-mail: MTCHBOXUSA@aol.com

Matchbox™ USA is run by Charlie Mack, the author of many books for the hobby. Charlie puts out a color newsletter once per month.

**11. Buy extras to swap and trade.** Matchbox™ is an international brand. Since the 1980s, many models are exclusive to different markets. Some models sold in the USA simply are not available in Europe and other areas of the world, and visa versa. There are exclusive models in the UK, Germany, Australia, Bulgaria, and other markets. Collecting is truly a worldwide endeavor now and you can establish trading partners around the world. Sending cars for trade is a fun and satisfying method to add to your collection.

**12. Explore the Internet.** Many collectors set up fantastic Web sites with great information and terrific photos. You will be amazed if you type "Matchbox™ Cars" in your Internet search engine. Spend a couple hours exploring the different sites. You will find many others that have the same interests you do.

**13. Open your toys.** Unlike Hot Wheels™ collectors, Matchbox™ collectors are not blister crazy for the most part. Yes, the mint-in-package model has a certain appeal, especially if it is more than thirty-five years old. Models produced since 1985 have very little collector value added by the blister card. So display your toys and enjoy the die-cast details out of the "plastic tombs."

**14. Price guides are only guides.** Remember that price guides are only guides, and you cannot use a value guide to argue with a seller. Careful study of reliable guides can develop your ability to determine fair prices.

Detailed price guides are useful as rarity guides. If the guide says car "X" in yellow is worth $10 and in red is worth $200, then you know the red one is very hard to find. You may have to pay $300 for the rare one or may find it at a toy show for $5 if you are lucky.

**15. Original boxes are valuable.** Original Matchbox™ boxes from the 1950s and 1960s are quite valuable. Some rare examples have sold for more than $500 with no toy. The value of a nice crisp 1950s box is easily $25. Any really nice box from the Regular Wheel era is probably worth $10 or more, so keep an eye out for empty boxes. The premium from vintage boxes is why you can find loose models for 50% less without boxes.

**16. Restoration parts are available.** Replacing the decals or other lost parts from your Matchbox™ vehicles can be a fun part of the hobby. Although some collectors look down upon this practice, this hobby is for you, so if you want to restore or customize some models, enjoy. But never sell a toy that you have restored without informing the buyer that the piece is not in original condition.

Two sources for replacement parts are:

**Steve Flowers** - www.model-supplies.co.uk

**Rick's Toy Box** - www.toydecals.com

# Regular Wheels

1 (A) Diesel Road Roller™, dark green, red MW, 1953, 1-7/8", MIMB **$120**

1 (B) Road Roller™, dark green, red MW, 1955, 2-3/8", MIMB **$90**

1 (C) Road Roller™, dark green, red MW, 1958, 2-1/4", MIMB **$90**

1 (D) Aveling Barford Road Roller™, dark green, red plastic wheels, 1962, 3", MIMB **$40**

1 (E) Mercedes Benz Lorry, mint green, orange plastic top, 1968, MIMB **$25**

2 (A) Dumper, green body, red dump, green painted MW, 1953, 1-5/8", MIMB
**$150**

2 (B) Dumper, green body, red dump, GPW, 1957, 1-7/8", MIMB **$85**

2 (C) Muir Hill Dumper, red body, green dump, "Laing", 1961, **$40**

2 (D) Mercedes Trailer, mint green, orange plastic top, 1968, MIMB **$20**

3 (A) Cement Mixer, blue, orange MW, 1953, MIMB **$85**

3 (B) Bedford Tipper, grey cab, red dump, GPW, 196l, MIMB **$70**

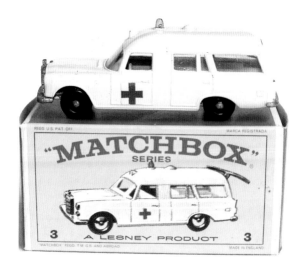

3 (C) Mercedes Benz "Binz" Ambulance, white, cross label, 1968, MIMB **$25**

4 (A) Massey Harris Tractor, red, fenders cast, MW, 1954, MIMB **$125**

4 (B) Massey Harris Tractor, red, no fenders, MW, 1957, MIMB **$100**

4 (C) Triumph Motorcycle & Sidecar, silver blue, 1960, MIMB **$125**

4 (D) Dodge Stake Truck, yellow, green stakes, 1967, MIMB **$25**

5 (A) London Bus, red body, "Buy Matchbox" label, MW, 1954, 2", MIMB
**$120**

5 (B) London Bus, red body, "Buy Matchbox" decal, MW, 1957, 2-1/4", MIMB
**$100**

5 (C) London Bus, red body, "Visco Static" decals, BPW, 1961, 2-9/16" MIMB
**$50**

5 (D) London Bus, red body, "Visco Static" decals, BPW, 1965, 2-3/4", MIMB
**$25**

6 (A) Quarry Truck, orange body, grey dump, MW, 1954, 2-1/8", MIMB **$90**

6 (B) Quarry Truck, yellow body, Euclid decal, BPW, 1957, 2-1/2", MIMB **$75**

6 (C) Euclid Quarry Truck, yellow body, BPW, 1964, MIMB **$30**

6 (D) Ford Pickup Truck, red body, white plastic top, 1968, MIMB **$30**

7 (A) Horse Drawn Milk Float, orange body, MW, white driver, 1954, MIMB
**$125**

7 (B) Ford Anglia, blue body, SPW, 1961, **$50**

7 (C) Ford Refuse Truck, orange body, silver loader, 1966, MIMB **$20**

8 (A) Caterpillar Tractor, orange body, 1955, 1-1/2", MIMB **$175**

8 (B) Caterpillar Tractor, yellow body, metal rollers, 1959, 1-5/8", MIMB
**$100**

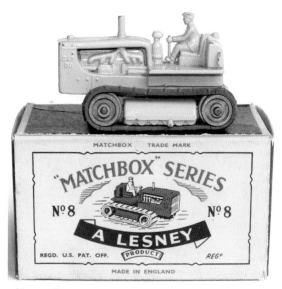

8 (C) Caterpillar Tractor, yellow body, metal rollers, 1961, 1-7/8", MIMB **$85**

8 (D) Caterpillar Tractor, yellow body, black plastic rollers, 1964, 2", MIMB **$40**

8 (E) Ford Mustang Fastback, white body, 1966, MIMB **$40**

9 (A) Dennis Fire Escape, red body, no number cast on base, MW, 1955, MIMB
**$100**

9 (B) Dennis Fire Escape, red body, "9" cast on base, MW, 1957, MIMB **$100**

9 (C) Merryweather Marquis Fire Engine, BPW, red body, 1959, MIMB **$45**

9 (D) Boat And Trailer, blue trailer, BPW, 1966, MIMB **$30**

10 (A) Mechanical Horse & Trailer, red body, grey back, 1955, 2-3/8", MIMB $80

10 (B) Mechanical Horse & Trailer, red body, tan trailer, MW, 1958, 2-15/16", MIMB **$75**

10 (C) Sugar Container Truck, blue body, BPW, 1961, MIMB **$70**

10 (D) Pipe Truck, red body, grey pipes, BPW, 1966, MIMB **$25**

11 (A) Road Tanker, red body, MW, 1955, 2", MIMB **$100**

11 (B) Road Tanker, red body, BPW, 1958, 2-1/2", MIMB **$125**

11 (C) Jumbo Crane, yellow body, red hook, BPW, 1965, MIMB **$30**

11 (D) Scaffold Truck, silver body, BPW, 1969, MIMB **$25**

12 (A) Land Rover, green body, MW, 1955, 1-3/4", MIMB **$75**

12 (B) Land Rover, green body, BPW, 1959, 2-1/4", **$50**

12 (C) Safari Land Rover, green body, BPW, 1965, MIMB **$25**

13 (A) Bedford Wreck Truck, tan body, red back, MW, 1955, 2", MIMB **$75**

13 (B) Bedford Wreck Truck, tan body, red back, 13 cast, MW, 1958, 2-1/8", MIMB **$75**

13 (C) Thames Wreck Truck, red body, silver hood, BPW, 196l, MIMB **$75**

13 (D) Dodge Wreck Truck, yellow cab, green back, red hood, BPW, 1965, MIMB **$35**

14 (A) Daimler Ambulance, cream body, cross decal, MW, 1956, 1-7/8", MIMB
**$70**

14 (B) Daimler Ambulance, cream body, cross decal, MW, 1958,
2-5/8", MIMB **$70**

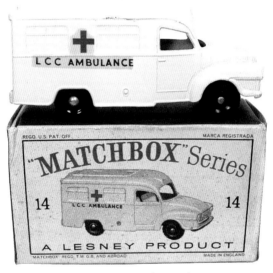

14 (C) Bedford Ambulance, white, BPW, 1962, MIMB **$50**

14 (D) Iso Grifo, blue, BPW, 1968, MIMB **$30**

15 (A) Prime Mover, orange, MW, 1956, MIMB **$85**

15 (B) Atlantic Prime Mover, orange, BPW, 1959, MIMB **$70**

15 (C) Refuse Truck, blue body, label, BPW, 1963, MIMB **$35**

15 (D) Volkswagen 1500 Saloon, white, decals, BPW, 1968, MIMB **$35**

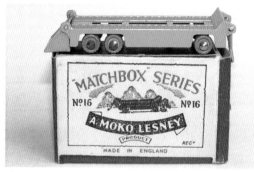

16 (A) Atlantic Trailer, tan, MW, 1956, 3-1/8", **$50**

16 (B) Atlantic Trailer, orange, BPW, 1957, 3-1/4", **$40**

16 (C) Scammell Mountaineer Snowplow, gray cab, orange tipper, GPW, 1964, MIMB **$125**

16 (D) Case Bulldozer, red, yellow top, 1969, MIMB **$30**

17 (A) Bedford Removals Van, green, MW, no 17 cast, 1956, MIMB **$100**

17 (C) Austin Taxi Cab, maroon, GPW, 1960, MIMB **$75**

17 (D) Hoveringham Tipper, red cab, orange back, 1963, MIMB **$40**

17 (E) Horse Box, red body, green box, BPW, 1969, MIMB **$25**

18 (A) Caterpillar Bulldozer, yellow, red blade, 1956, 1-7/8", MIMB **$100**

18 (B) Caterpillar Bulldozer, yellow, yellow blade, 1958, 2", MIMB **$85**

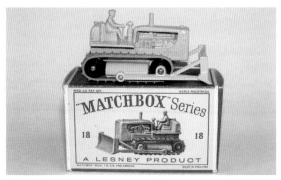

18 (C) Caterpillar Bulldozer, yellow, black rollers, 1961, 2-1/4", MIMB **$75**

18 (D) Bulldozer, yellow, black rollers 1964, 2-3/8", MIMB **$35**

18 (E) Field Car, yellow, black base, green wheels, 1969, MIMB **$25**

19 (A) MG TC, cream, MW, 1956, 2", MIMB **$100**

19 (B) MGA , white, MW, 1958, 2-1/4", MIMB **$100**

19 (C) Aston Martin Racing Car, green, white driver, "19" decal, 1961, MIMB
$85

19 (D) Lotus Racing Car, orange, 3 decals, 1966, MIMB **$45**

20 (A) Stake Truck, maroon, MW, 1956, MIMB **$75**

20 (B) ERF Truck, blue, "Ever Ready" decals, GPW, 1959, **$85**

20 (C) Chevrolet Impala Taxi Cab, yellow, unpainted base, BPW, 1965, MIMB
**$35**

21 (A) Long Distance Coach, light green body, "London to Glasgow" decals, MW, 1956, 2-1/4", MIMB **$100**

21 (B) Long Distance Coach, light green body, "London to Glasgow" decals, MW, 1958, 2-5/8", MIMB **$125**

21 (C) Commer Milk Float, green body, cow decal, white load, BPW, 1961, MIMB **$60**

21 (D) Foden Concrete Truck, red base, yellow cab, 1968, MIMB **$20**

22 (A) Vauxhall Cresta, red, white roof, MW, 1956, MIMB **$50**

22 (B) 1958 Vauxhall Cresta, pink and grey, BPW, 1958, **$100**

22 (C) Pontiac Gran Prix Sports Coupe, red body, BPW, 1964, MIMB **$40**

23 (A) Berkeley Cavalier Trailer, light blue, no number on base, MW, 1956, MIMB **$75**

23 (B) Berkeley Cavalier Trailer, light green, 23 on base, GPW, 1958, MIMB **$75**

23 (C) Bluebird Dauphine Trailer, tan body, SPW, 1960, MIMB **$75**

23 (D) Trailer Caravan, pink body, BPW, 1965, MIMB **$30**

24 (A) Weatherhill Hydraulic Excavator, 1956, 2-3/8", MIMB **$45**

24 (B) Weatherhill Hydraulic Excavator, yellow body, BPW, 1959, 2-5/8", MIMB **$45**

24 (C) Rolls Royce Silver Shadow, red body, BPW, 1967, MIMB **$25**

25 (A) Dunlop Van, blue body, MW, "Dunlop" decals, 1956, MIMB **$100**

25 (B) Volkswagen 1200 Sedan, light blue body, GPW, 1960, MIMB **$120**

25 (C) BP Tanker, green base, yellow cab, "BP" decals, 1964, MIMB **$40**

25 (D) Ford Cortina, tan body, BPW, 1968, MIMB **$25**

26 (A) Concrete Truck, orange body, MW, 1956, 1-3/4", MIMB **$65**

26 (B) Foden Concrete Truck, orange body, GPW, 1961, 2-1/2", MIMB **$60**

26 (C) G.M.C. Tipper Truck, red body, silver dump, 1968, MIMB **$25**

27 (A) Bedford Lowloader, green body, tan trailer, MW, 1956, 3-1/8", MIMB
**$100**

27 (C) Cadillac Sixty Special, silver body, white roof, SPW, 1960, MIMB **$95**

27 (D) Mercedes Benz 230SL, white body, BPW, 1966, MIMB **$30**

28 (A) Bedford Compressor Truck, orange body, MW, 1956, MIMB **$65**

28 (B) Thames Compressor Truck, yellow body, BPW, 1959, MIMB **$50**

28 (C) Mk.10 Jaguar, brown body, BPW, 1964, MIMB **$45**

28 (D) Mack Dump Truck, orange body, red hubs, BPW, 1968, MIMB **$35**

29 (A) Bedford Milk Delivery Van, tan body, GPW, 1956, MIMB **$110**

29 (B) Austin A55 Cambridge Sedan, green body, SPW, 1961, MIMB **$80**

29 (C) Fire Pumper, red body, BPW, 1966, **$30**

30 (A) Ford Prefect, tan body, MW, 1956, MIMB **$65**

30 (B) Magiruz-Deutz Crane Truck, silver body, metal hook, SPW, MW, 1961, MIMB **$75**

30 (C) 8-Wheel Crane Truck, green body, yellow hook, BPW, 1965, MIMB **$30**

31 (A) Ford Station Wagon, yellow body, MW, 1957, MIMB **$75**

31 (B) Ford Station Wagon, green body, pink roof, SPW, 1960, MIMB **$75**

31 (C) Lincoln Continental, light green body, BPW, 1964, MIMB **$30**

32 (A) Jaguar XKI40 Coupe, red body, GPW, 1957, MIMB **$125**

32 (B) Jaguar XKE, red body, green windows, BPW, 1962, MIMB **$50**

32 (C) Leyland Petrol Tanker, green cab, white tank, "BP" decals, 1968, MIMB **$20**

33 (A) Ford Zodiac MKII Sedan, dark green, MW, 1957, MIMB **$75**

33 (B) Ford Zephyr 6 MK III, blue green body, BPW, 1963, MIMB **$30**

33 (C) Lamborghini Miura, yellow, red interior, BPW, 1969, MIMB **$25**

34 (A) Volkswagen Microvan, blue body, GPW, 1957, MIMB **$80**

34 (B) Volkswagen Camper, light green body, BPW, 1962, 2-3/5", MIMB **$70**

34 (D) Volkswagen Camper, silver body, low roof, BPW, 1967, MIMB **$30**

35 (A) Marshall Horse Box, red body, tan back, GPW, 1957, MIMB **$70**

35 (B) Snow Trac Tractor, red body, "Snow Trac" decals, white treads, 1964,
MIMB **$35**

36 (A) Austin A50, blue body, GPW, 1957, MIMB **$80**

36 (B) Lambretta Scooter & Sidecar, green body, BPW, 1961, MIMB **$125**

36 (C) Opel Diplomat, gold body, BPW, 1966, MIMB **$20**

37 (A) Coca-Cola Lorry, orange body, uneven case load, no base, 1956, MIMB
**$125**

37 (B) Dodge Cattle Truck, yellow body, metal base, 1966, MIMB **$25**

38 (A) Karrier Refuse Collector, gray body, GPW, 1957, **$75**

38 (B) Vauxhall Victor Estate Car, yellow body, green interior, BPW, 1963, MIMB **$50**

38 (C) Honda Motorcycle & Trailer, yellow trailer, blue bike, 1967, MIMB **$35**

39 (A) Ford Zodiac Convertible, salmon body, GPW, 1957, MIMB **$120**

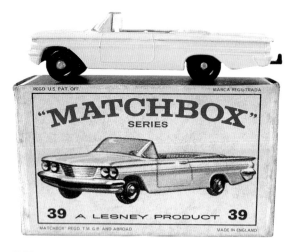

39 (B) Pontiac Convertible, yellow body, BPW, 1962, MIMB $85

39 (C) Ford Tractor, blue body, yellow hood, 1967, MIMB **$30**

40 (C) Hay Trailer, blue body, yellow stakes, 1967, MIMB **$20**

40 (A) Bedford Tipper Truck, red body, tan dumper, GPW, 1957, MIMB **$80**

40 (B) Leyland Royal Tiger Coach, metallic blue, BPW, 1961, MIMB **$35**

41 (A) D-Type Jaguar, green body, MW, "41" decal, 1957, 2-3/16", MIMB **$100**

41 (B) D-Type Jaguar, green body, red wheels, "41" decal, 1960, 2-7/16", MIMB **$650**

41 (C) Ford GT, white body, "6" decal, yellow wheels, 1965, MIMB **$30**

42 (A) Bedford Evening News Van, yellow body, "Evening News" decals, BPW, 1957, MIMB **$125**

42 (B) Studebaker Lark Wagonaire, blue body, BPW, 1965, MIMB **$50**

42 (C) Iron Fairy Crane, red body, yellow boom, 1969, MIMB **$25**

43 (A) Hillman Minx, light blue, cream roof, GPW, 1958, MIMB **$85**

43 (B) Aveling Barford Tractor Shovel, yellow body, red shovel, BPW, 1962, MIMB **$60**

43 (C) Pony Trailer, yellow body, green base, BPW, 1968, MIMB **$30**

44 (A) Rolls Royce Silver Cloud, blue body, GPW, 1958, MIMB **$75**

44 (B) Rolls Royce Phantom V, tan body, BPW, 1964, MIMB **$50**

44 (C) G.M.C. Refrigerator Truck, red body, green box, 1967, MIMB **$25**

45 (A) Vauxhall Victor, yellow body, no windows, GPW, 1958, MIMB **$90**

45 (B) Ford Corsair With Boat, yellow body, GPW, 1965, MIMB **$70**

46 (A) Morris Minor 1000, blue body, GPW, 1958, MIMB **$125**

46 (B) Pickfords Removal Van, green body, "Pickfords" decal, BPW, 1960, MIMB **$65**

46 (C) Mercedes Benz 300 SE, green body, BPW, 1968, MIMB **$25**

47 (A) 1-Ton Trojan Van, red body, "Brooke Bond Tea" decals, MW, 1958, MIMB **$80**

47 (B) Commer Ice Cream Canteen, blue body, white plastic load, BPW, 1963, MIMB **$60**

47 (C) DAF Tipper Container Truck, silver body, yellow box, grey plastic top, 1968, MIMB **$35**

48 (A) Meteor Sports Boat & Trailer, blue body, tan top, MW, 1958, MIMB **$75**

48 (B) Sports Boat & Trailer, white body, red top, BPW, 1961, MIMB **$75**

48 (C) Dodge Dumper Truck, red body, BPW, 1966, MIMB **$35**

49 (A) M3 Personnel Carrier, green body, grey treads, BPW, 1958, MIMB **$60**

49 (B) Mercedes Unimog, tan body, green base, 1967, MIMB **$40**

50 (A) Commer Pickup, red and gray, BPW, 1958, MIMB **$150**

50 (C) Ford Kennel Truck, green body, white grille, 1969, MIMB **$35**

50 (B) John Deere Tractor, green body, BPW, 1964, MIMB **$45**

51 (B) John Deere Trailer, green body, GPW, 1964, MIMB **$25**

51 (A) Albion Chieftan, yellow body, "Blue Circle Portland Cement" decals, GPW, 1958, MIMB **$100**

51 (C) 8-Wheel Tipper, yellow body, silver tipper, "Douglas" labels, 1969, MIMB **$40**

52 (A) Maserati 4CLT Racer, yellow, "52" decals, 1958, MIMB **$125**

52 (B) BRM Racing Car, red body, "5" decal, 1965, MIMB **$45**

53 (A) Aston Martin, green body, GPW, 1958, MIMB **$100**

53 (B) Mercedes Benz 220SE, maroon body, BPW, 1963, MIMB **$45**

53 (C) Ford Zodiac MK IV, blue body, BPW, 1968, MIMB **$20**

54 (A) Saracen Personnel Carrier, green body, BPW, 1958, MIMB **$60**

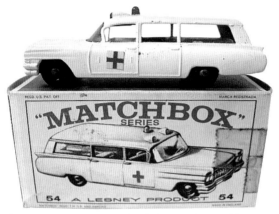

54 (B) S & S Cadillac Ambulance, white body, BPW, 1965, MIMB **$40**

55 (A) D.U.K.W., green body, MW, 1958, MIMB **$80**

55 (B) Ford Fairlane Police Car, dark blue body, BPW, 1963, MIMB **$275**

55 (C) Ford Galaxie Police Car, white body, red light, BPW, 1966, MIMB **$45**

55 (D) Mercury Police Car, white body, blue light, BPW, 1968, MIMB **$35**

56 (A) Trolley Bus, red body, "Peardrax" decals, MW, 1958, MIMB **$85**

56 (B) Fiat 1500, green body, BPW, 1965, MIMB **$25**

57 (A) Wolseley 1500, light green, GPW, 1958, MIMB **$75**

57 (B) Chevrolet Impala, metallic blue, SPW, 1961, MIMB **$120**

57 (C) Land Rover Fire Truck, red, "Kent Fire Brigade" decals, BPW, 1966, MIMB **$30**

58 (A) BEA Coach, blue body, "British European Airways" decals, GPW, 1958, MIMB **$80**

58 (B) Drott Excavator, red body, black rollers, 1962, MIMB **$60**

58 (C) DAF Girder Truck, white body, red girders, 1968, MIMB **$25**

59 (A) Ford Thames Van, light green, "Singer" decals, GPW, 1958, MIMB **$90**

59 (B) Ford Fairlane Fire Chief Car, red body, "Fire Chief" decals, BPW, 1963, MIMB **$85**

59 (C) Ford Galaxie Fire Chief Car, red body, "Fire Chief" and shield decals, BPW, 1966, MIMB **$40**

60 (A) Morris 32 Pickup, blue body, "Builders Supply" decals, SPW, 1958, MIMB **$75**

60 (B) Site Hut Truck, blue body, BPW, 1966, MIMB **$25**

61 (A) Ferret Scout Car, green body, BPW, 1959, MIMB **$70**

61 (B) Alvis Stalwart, white body, green plastic hubs, 1966, MIMB **$40**

62 (A) General Service Lorry, green body, BPW, 1959, MIMB **$90**

62 (B) TV Service Van, tan body, "Rentaset" decal, BPW, 1963, MIMB **$70**

62 (C) Mercury Cougar, green body, BPW, 1968, MIMB **$35**

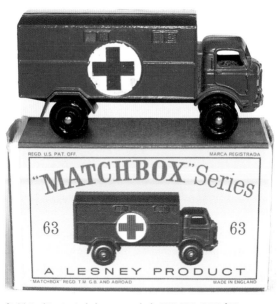

63 (A) Ford Service Ambulance, green body, BPW, 1959, MIMB **$90**

63 (B) Foamite Crash Tender, red body, BPW, 1964, **$50**

63 (C) Dodge Crane Truck, yellow body, red hook, 1968, MIMB **$25**

64 (A) Scammell Breakdown Truck, green body, BPW, 1959, MIMB **$80**

64 (B) MG 1100, green body, BPW, 1966, MIMB **$20**

65 (A) Jaguar 3.4 Litre Saloon, metallic blue, GPW, 1959, MIMB **$150**

65 (B) Jaguar 3.4 Litre Saloon, maroon body, BPW, 1962, 2-5/8", MIMB **$55**

65 (C) Claas Combine Harvester, red body, BPW, 1967, MIMB **$35**

66 (A) Citroen DS19, yellow body, GPW, 1959, MIMB **$120**

66 (B) Harley-Davidson Motorcycle & Sidecar, bronze body, BPW, 1962, MIMB
**$200**

66 (C) Greyhound Bus, silver body, yellow windows, BPW, 1967, MIMB **$40**

67 (A) Saladin Armoured Car, green body, BPW, 1959, **$60**

67 (B) Volkswagen 1600TL, orange body, BPW, 1967, MIMB **$40**

68 (A) Austin MKII Radio Truck, green body, BPW, 1959, MIMB **$75**

68 (B) Mercedes Coach, orange body, BPW, 1965, MIMB **$25**

69 (A) Commer 30 CWT Van, maroon body, "Nestle's" decal, GPW, 1959,
**$100**

69 (B) Hatra Tractor Shovel, yellow body, BPW, 1965, MIMB **$50**

70 (B) Ford Grit Spreader Truck, red body, yellow box, BPW, 1966, MIMB **$25**

71 (A) Austin 200 Gallon Water Truck, green body, model came with button, BPW, 1959, MIMB **$75**

71 (B) Jeep Gladiator Pickup, red body, BPW, 1964, MIMB **$60**

71 (C) Ford Heavy Wreck Truck, red and white body, "Esso" decals, BPW, 1968, MIMB **$40**

72 (A) Fordson Tractor, blue body, GPW, 1959, MIMB **$75**

72 (B) Standard Jeep, yellow body, BPW, 1966, MIMB **$40**

73 (B) Ferrari F1 Racing Car, red body, white driver, 1962, MIMB **$50**

73 (C) Mercury Station Wagon, green body, BPW, 1968, MIMB **$30**

74 (A) Mobile Refreshment Canteen, grey body, "Refreshments" decals, 1959, MIMB **$120**

74 (B) Daimler Bus, biege body, "Esso" labels, BPW, 1966, MIMB **$25**

75 (A) Ford Thunderbird, pink and white body, SPW, 1960, MIMB **$100**

75 (B) Ferrari Berlinetta, green body, spoked wheels, 1965, MIMB **$45**

# Rare Ones

As with all collectables, some models are more rare than others. The photos in this chapter suggest models to look for. Some are hard to find. Some are just impossible. If you are lucky maybe you can find one at a bargain price.

**41 Ford GT**

The model in yellow was only available in gift sets. This model sells for more than **$125** in mint condition. The model with the red hubs is very rare. Expect to pay **$400+** if mint.

**46 Pickford Van**
This Beales Bealson was a promotion for a store in England. Very short production run. It sells for **$800** in mint condition.

**62 TV Service Van**

This model with gray plastic wheels is very rare. The value is **$500+**.

**39 Ford Tractor**
This orange model is very hard to find and worth **$125** in mint condition.

### 30 6-Wheel Crane
This model in tan is one of the rarest Matchbox™ models. It has sold more than once for **$10,000+.**

Any regular wheel model in one of the early blister packs as shown is worth a **$50** premium over a similar model that is MIB.

This model in two-tone blue is very rare. It is valued at over **$2000.**

**46 Morris Minor**
This model was released in very limited numbers. It is probably a pre-
production color trial model. The value is **$2000+.**

### 31 Ford Fairlane Station Wagon

This model was released quite briefly in the yellow color of the earlier wagon. The normal green color is shown. Expect to pay **$350** for a yellow one.

### 41 D-Type Jaguar

The larger D-Type model was released briefly with red-hubbed wheels. The model is valued at **$700+.** Look for any model that has a number other than the normal "41." These odd numbered models are worth more than double the regular issue.

**26 Foden Concrete Truck**
The model usually has an orange mixer. Find the mixer in gray and the
value is **$500 or more.**

**39 Ford Zodiac**

This model normally comes with a turquoise interior. Find the rare one with a tan interior and expect to pay **$700+.**

The regular wheel Ferrari in the Superfast™ color of red is valued at **$700+.**

# Lesney Superfast™

1 (A) Mercedes Truck, gold body, yellow top, 1970, MIMB **$25**

1 (B) Mod Rod, yellow body, scorpion decal on hood, 1971, MIMB **$25**

1 (C) Dodge Challenger, red body, white top, chrome interior, 1976, MIMB **$15**

1 (D) Dodge Challenger, orange body, black interior, "Revin Rebel" design, 1982, MIMB **$12**

2 (A) Mercedes Trailer, gold body, yellow top, 1970, MIMB **$15**

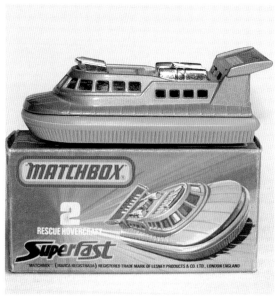

2 (C) Hovercraft, green body, "Rescue" decal on tail, 1976, MIMB **$12**

2 (D) S 2 Jet, brown body, yellow wings, 1981, MIMB **$12**

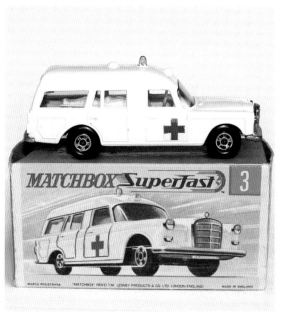

3 (A) Mercedes Benz "Binz" Ambulance, white body, cross label, 1970, MIMB
**$25**

3 (B) Monteverdi Hai, orange body, "3" decal on hood, 1973, MIMB **$15**

4 (A) Stake Truck, yellow body, green stakes, 1970, MIMB **$20**

4 (B) Gruesome Twosome, red body, purple windows, 1971, MIMB **$15**

4 (C) Pontiac Firebird, blue body, yellow windows, 1975, MIMB **$15**

4 (D) '57 Chevy, purple body, chrome interior, 1979, MIMB **$15**

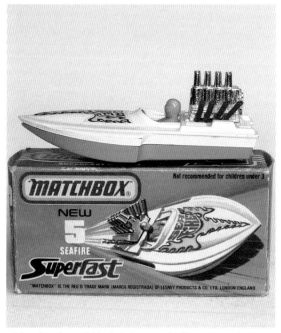

5 (B) Seafire, white with blue body, "Sea Fire" decals, 1975, MIMB **$12**

5 (C) Jeep / U.S. Mail Truck, blue body, white top, "US MAIL" tampo, 1978, MIMB **$12**

6 (A) Ford Pick-Up, red body, white grille, 1970, MIMB **$25**

6 (B) Mercedes 350 SL, bronze body, white top, 1976, MIMB **$12**

7 (B) Hairy Hustler, bronze body, "5" labels, 1971, MIMB **$15**

7 (C) VW Golf, silver body, red interior, "GOLF" tampo, 1976, MIMB **$12**

7 (D) Romping Rabbit, white body, "Rompin Rabbit" design, 1982, MIMB **$10**

8 (A) Mustang, red orange body, white interior, 1970, MIMB **$50**

8 (B) Wildcat Dragster, orange body, yellow and orange "Wild Cat" decals, 1971, MIMB **$20**

8 (C) De Tomaso Pantera, blue body, "17" tampo, white stripes, 1975, MIMB **$12**

8 (D) Rover 3500, bronze body, 1982, MIMB **$12**

9 (A) Boat & Trailer, blue and white plastic boat, blue trailer, 1970, MIMB
**$20**

9 (B) Amx Javelin, green body, 1972, MIMB **$15**

9 (D) Fiat Abarth, white body, red and orange stripes, "45 Matchbox" tampo, 1982, MIMB **$12**

10 (A) Pipe Truck, orange body, yellow pipes, 1970, MIMB **$18**

10 (B) Mustang Piston Popper, blue body, 1973, MIMB **$15**

10 (C) Plymouth Gran Fury, black and white body, "Police" tampo, 1979, MIMB **$12**

11 (B) Flying Bug, red body, cross decal on hood, gray windows, 1972, MIMB
**$15**

11 (C) Car Transporter, orange body, tan trailer, 1976, MIMB **$12**

12 (A) Land Rover Safari, gold body, 1970, MIMB **$30**

12 (B) Setra Coach, green body, white roof, 1971, MIMB **$13**

12 (D) Citroen CX, blue body, black base, 1979, MIMB **$10**

12 (E) Pontiac Firebird SE, red body, silver base, 1982, MIMB **$10**

13 (A) Dodge Wreck Truck, yellow body, green back, "BP" labels, 1970, MIMB
**$40**

13 (B) Baja Buggy, green body, red interior, flower decal on hood, 1971,
MIMB **$15**

14 (A) Iso Grifo, light blue body, white interior, 1969, MIMB **$20**

14 (B) Mini-Ha-Ha, red body, target label, blue windows, 1975, MIMB **$15**

14 (C) Rallye Royale, grey body, blue stripe on hood, "14" tampo, 1981, MIMB **$12**

14 (D) Articulated Tanker, red body, white tanker, "ELF" labels, 1982, MIMB
**$15**

15 (B) Fork Lift Truck, red body, yellow hooks, "Lansing Bagnall" labels, 1972, MIMB **$15**

15 (C) Hi Ho Silver, gray body, "Hi Ho Silver" and hat tampo, 1981, MIMB
**$15**

16 (A) Badger, bronze body, chrome antennae, 1974, MIMB **$13**

16 (B) Pontiac Firebird, gold body, firebird label on hood, 1979, MIMB **$15**

17 (B) The Londoner, red, "Berger Paints" label, 1972, MIMB **$12**

17 (C) London Bus, red, "Laker Skytrain" label, 1982, **$12**

18 (A) Field Car, green body, tan top, "A" label, 1970, MIMB **$25**

18 (B) Hondarora, red body, black seat, "Honda" label, 1975, MIMB **$12**

19 (B) Road Dragster, red body, "8" labels, 1971, MIMB **$20**

19 (C) Cement Truck, red body, gray barrel, green windows, 1976, MIMB **$13**

19 (D) Peterbilt Cement Truck, green body, orange barrel, "Big Pete" and man tampo design, 1982, MIMB **$15**

20 (A) Lamborghini Marzal, red, 1969, MIMB **$20**

21 (A) Foden Concrete Truck, yellow body and barrel, red base, 1970, MIMB
$35

21 (B) Rod Roller, yellow body, red seat, star and flames decal on hood, 1973, MIMB **$15**

21 (C) Renault 5 TL, blue body, gray interior, 1978, MIMB **$10**

22 (A) Pontiac GP Sports Coupé, purple body, 1970, MIMB **$50**

22 (C) Blaze Buster, red body, yellow ladder, "Fire" decals, 1975, MIMB **$13**

23 (A) Volkswagen Camper, blue body, orange top, 1970, MIMB **$35**

23 (B) Atlas Dump, blue body, orange dump, stripe decal, 1975, MIMB **$15**

23 (C) GT 350, white body, "GT 350" tampo, 1981, MIMB **$25**

24 (A) Rolls Royce Silver Shadow, red body, white interior, 1970, MIMB **$25**

24 (B) Team Matchbox™, red body, "8" label, 1973, MOC **$12**

24 (C) Shunter, green body, red base, "Rail Freight" label, 1978, MIMB **$8**

24 (D) Datsun 280 ZX, black body, red "Datsun 280ZX" tampo, 1981, MIMB
**$15**

25 (A) Ford Cortina Mk II, blue body, white interior, 1970, MIMB **$30**

25 (B) Mod Tractor, red body, yellow seat, 1972, MIMB **$13**

25 (C) Flat Car, black base, tan and red car, "N.Y.K." labels, 1978, MIMB **$8**

25 (D) Toyota Celica, light blue body, white "78" stripes, 1981, MIMB **$13**

26 (B) Big Banger, red body, "Big Banger" decal, 1972, MIMB **$18**

26 (C) Site Dumper, yellow body, black seat, 1976, MIMB **$13**

26 (D) Cosmic Blues, white, blue "Cosmic Blues" tampo, 1981, MIMB **$13**

26 (E) Volvo Cable Truck, orange body, black and grey cable spools, 1982, MIMB **$18**

27 (B) Lamborghini Countach, red body, green and black, "8" tampo, 1973, MIMB **$15**

27 (C) Swing Wing, red body, white base and wings, 1981, MIMB **$12**

28 (A) Dump Truck, green body, 1970, MIMB **$20**

28 (B) Stoat, green body, brown driver, 1974, MIMB **$18**

28 (D) Formula 5000, metallic tan body, white and black "8" design, 1981, MIMB **$13**

29 (A) Fire Pumper Truck, red body, blue windows, 1970, MIMB **$40**

29 (B) Racing Mini, red body, "29" decals, 1971, MIMB **$25**

29 (C) Tractor Shovel, yellow body, red shovel, 1976, MIMB **$16**

30 (B) Beach Buggy, purple body, yellow interior, yellow splotches, 1971, MIMB **$22**

30 (C) Swamp Rat, green body, tan driver, "Swamp Rats" label, 1976, MIMB
**$15**

30 (D) Articulated Truck, blue body, silver dump, 1981, MIMB **$20**

30 (E) Peterbilt Quarry Truck, yellow body, gray dump, "Dirty Dumper" tampo, 1982, MIMB **$12**

31 (C) Caravan, white body, yellow door, orange stripe decals, 1977, MIMB
**$13**

31 (D) Mazda RX 7, blue body, white interior, 1981, MIMB **$15**

32 (A) Petrol Tanker, green cab, white tanker, "BP" labels, 1970, MIMB **$30**

32 (B) Maserati Bora, purple body, yellow interior, "8" label, 1972, MIMB
**$15**

32 (D) Atlas Excavator, red body and shovel, black base and boom, 1981, MIMB **$15**

33 (A) Lamborghini Miura, gold body, white interior, 1969, MIMB **$20**

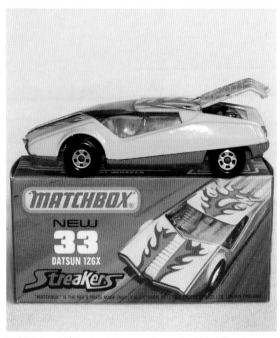

33 (B) Datsun 126 X, yellow body orange base, red and black flame tampo, 1973, MIMB **$15**

33 (C) Honda Police Motorcycle, black cycle, blue rider, "Police" decals, 1977, MIMB **$18**

34 (B) Vantastic, orange body, white base, "34" label, 1975, MIMB **$18**

34 (C) Chevy Pro Stocker, white body, blue "34" lightning tampo, 1981, MIMB **$25**

35 (A) Merryweather Fire Engine, red body, white ladder, "London Fire Service" labels, 1970, MIMB **$30**

35 (B) Fandango, red body, blue spinner, "35" label, 1975, MIMB **$15**

35 (D) Volvo Zoo Truck, red body, blue cage, 1982, MIMB **$25**

36 (A) Opel Diplomat, gold body, chrome engine, 1970, MIMB **$25**

36 (B) Hot Rod Draguar, red body, "draguar" label, 1971, MIMB **$25**

36 (C) Formula 5000, orange body, blue driver, "5000" label, 1978, MIMB
**$15**

37 (A) Cattle Truck, orange body, gray box, 1970, MIMB **$30**

37 (B) Soopa Coopa, purple body, flower label, 1972, MIMB **$13**

37 (C) Skip Truck, red body, yellow skip, 1976, MIMB **$13**

38 (A) Honda Motor Cycle Trailer, orange trailer, green bike, "Honda" labels, 1970, MIMB **$35**

38 (B) The Stingeroo Chopper, purple body, blue handlebars, 1972, MIMB
**$25**

38 (C) Jeep, green body, black gun, star tampo, 1976, MIMB **$18**

38 (D) Camper, red body, tan top, 1980, MIMB **$15**

38 (E) Model A Ford, blue body, "Champion" labels, 1982, MIMB **$12**

39 (B) Rolls-Royce Silver Shadow II, burgundy body, white interior, 1979, MIMB **$14**

39 (C) Toyota Supra, white body, red "41" stripes tampo, black hatch, 1983, MIMB **$12**

40 (A) Vauxhall Guildsman, pink body, green windows, star decal, 1971, **$14**

40 (B) Horse-Box, yellow body, brown box, white door, 1977, MIMB **$12**

41 (A) Ford GT, red body, "blue 6" label, 1970, MIMB **$35**

41 (B) Siva Spyder, blue body, stars and stripes tampo, 1972, MIMB **$12**

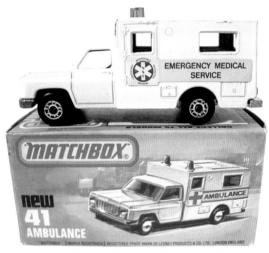

41 (C) Ambulance, white body, "Emergency Medical Service" labels, 1977, MIMB **$13**

41 (D) Kenworth Aerodyne, red body, white and black stripes tampo, 1982, MIMB **$10**

42 (B) Tyre Fryer, blue body, yellow interior, 1972, MIMB **$15**

42 (C) Mercedes Container Truck, yellow body and container, "Deutsche Bundespost" Labels, 1977, MIMB **$25**

42 (D) 1957 Thunderbird, white body, red stripes, "Thunder Bird" tampo, 1982, MIMB **$13**

43 (A) Pony Trailer, yellow body, green base, 1970, **$25**

43 (C) 0-4-0 Steam Loco, red body, black base, "4543" labels, 1978, MIMB
**$10**

43 (D) Peterbilt, black body, red and white tampo, 1982, MIMB **$12**

44 (A) G.M.C. Refrigerator Truck, yellow body, red container, 1970, MIMB
**$30**

44 (B) Boss Mustang, yellow body, black hood, 1972, MIMB **$18**

44 (D) 4 X 4 Chevy Van, green body, "Ridin High" horse tampo, 1982, MIMB
**$10**

45 (A) Ford Group 6, green body, "7" label, 1970, MIMB **$18**

45 (B) BMW 3.0 CSL, orange body, "BMW" label, 1976, MIMB **$15**

46 (A) Mercedes 300 SE, gold body, 1970, MIMB **$30**

46 (C) Ford Tractor, blue body, yellow plow, 1978, MIMB **$12**

46 (D) Hot Chocolate, bronze and black body, 1982, MIMB **$15**

47 (A) DAF Tipper Container Truck, silver body, yellow tipper, 1970, MIMB
**$30**

47 (B) Beach Hopper, blue body, orange interior, 1974, MIMB **$15**

47 (D) SS 100 Jaguar, red body, tan interior, 1982, MIMB **$13**

48 (A) Dumper Truck, blue body, yellow dumper, 1970, MIMB **$25**

48 (B) Pi-Eyed Piper, blue body, "8" stripes label, 1972, MIMB **$15**

48 (C) Sambron Jacklift, yellow body and lift, 1977, MIMB **$12**

48 (E) Unimog, yellow body and plow, "Rescue" tampo, 1982, MIMB **$10**

49 (A) Unimog, metallic blue body, maroon base, 1970, MIMB **$25**

49 (B) Chop Suey Chopper, magenta body, red handlebars, 1973, MIMB **$18**

50 (A) Kennel Truck, light green body, white grille, 1970, MIMB **$30**

50 (B) Articulated Truck, yellow body, blue dumper, yellow decals, 1973, MIMB **$13**

50 (C) Harley-Davidson Sportster, bronze body, tan driver, 1980, MIMB **$20**

51 (A) 8-Wheel Tipper, yellow body, silver dumper, "Pointer" decals, 1970, MIMB **$25**

51 (B) Citroen S.M., red body, 1972, MIMB **$14**

51 (C) Combine Harvester, red body, yellow blades, 1978, MIMB **$12**

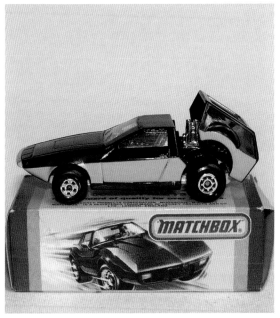

51 (D) Midnight Magic, black and silver body, chrome interior, 1981, MIMB
**$10**

52 (A) Dodge Charger MK III, red body, 1970, MIMB **$18**

53 (A) Ford Zodiac MK IV, green body, 1970, MIMB **$25**

53 (B) Tanzara, orange body, green windows, 1977, MIMB **$15**

53 (C) Jeep CJ 6, red body, tan top, yellow interior, 1977, MIMB **$15**

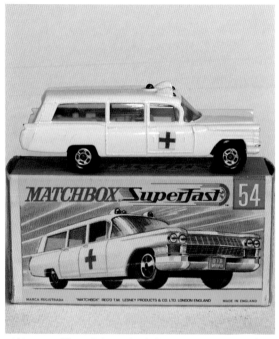

54 (A) S & S Cadillac Ambulance, white body, cross labels, 1970, MIMB **$45**

54 (C) Personnel Carrier, green body, tan men, 1976, MIMB **$13**

54 (D) Mobile Home, tan body, brown door, 1980, MIMB **$15**

54 (E) NASA Tracking Vehicle, white body, chrome antennae, "NASA Space Shuttle" tampo, 1982, MIMB **$13**

55 (A) Mercury, white body, red light, "Police" shield labels, 1970, MIMB **$25**

55 (C) Hellraiser, blue body, stars and stripes label, 1975, MIMB **$15**

55 (D) Ford Cortina, dark red body, black stripe, white interior, 1979, MIMB
**$13**

56 (A) BMC 1800 Pininfarina, gold body, 1969, MIMB **$15**

56 (B) Hi-Tailer, white body, red base, yellow driver, "Martini Racing 7" labels, 1974, MIMB **$13**

56 (D) Peterbilt Tanker, blue body, white tanker, red "Milk's The One" tampo, 1982, MIMB **$10**

57 (A) Land Rover Fire Truck, red body, blue windows, "Kent Fire Brigade" shield labels, 1970, MIB **$50**

57 (B) Trailer Caravan, beige body, orange top, brown stripe, 1971, MIMB
**$20**

57 (C) Wild Life Truck, yellow body, red windows, "Ranger" elephant label, 1973, MIMB **$20**

58 (A) DAF Girder Truck, green body, red girders, 1970, MIMB **$25**

58 (B) Woosh-N-Push, purple body, off white interior, "2" label, 1972, MIMB
**$10**

58 (C) Faun Dump Truck, yellow body, black base, 1976, MIMB **$13**

59 (A) Ford Galaxie, red body, "Fire Chief" shield labels, 1970, MIMB **$25**

59 (B) Mercury, red body, "Fire Chief" helmet labels, 1971, MIMB **$20**

59 (D) Porsche 928, blue body, brown interior, 1980, MIMB **$14**

60 (B) Lotus Super Seven, orange body, black interior, flame label, 1971,
MIMB **$15**

60 (D) Mustang Piston Popper, yellow body, red windows, "60" tampo, 1982, MIMB **$13**

61 (B) Wreck Truck, red body, white booms, red hooks, 1978, MIMB **$13**

61 (C) Peterbilt, orange body, "Eddie's Wrecker" tampo, 1982, MIMB **$10**

62 (A) Mercury Cougar, green body, red interior, 1970, MIMB **$30**

62 (C) Renault 17 TL, red body, black base, green windows, "6" hood label, 1974, MIMB **$15**

63 (A) Dodge Crane Truck, yellow body, green windows, yellow hook, 1970, MIMB **$20**

63 (B) Freeway Gas Tanker, red cab, white tanker, "Burmah" labels, 1973, MIMB **$13**

64 (A) MG 1100, blue body, white interior, 1970, MIMB **$40**

64 (B) Slingshot Dragster, blue body, "9" flame decal, 1971, MIMB **$15**

64 (D) Caterpillar Tractor, yellow body, tan top, black treads, 1979, MIMB
**$13**

65 (B) Airport Coach, blue body, white top, yellow windows, 1977, "American Airlines" decals, MIMB **$15**

66 (A) Greyhound Coach, silver body, yellow windows, "Greyhound" decals, 1970, MIMB **$30**

66 (C) Ford Transit, orange body, green windows, tan load, 1977, MIMB **$15**

67 (A) Volkswagen 1600 TL, purple body, white interior, 1970, MIMB **$30**

67 (C) Datsun 260 Z 2 + 2, purple body, clear windows, 1978, MIMB **$13**

68 (C) Chevy Van, orange body, white and blue stripes, blue windows, 1982, MIMB **$15**

69 (A) Rolls Royce Silver Shadow Coupé, blue body, 1969, MIMB **$25**

70 (A) Grit Spreader, red body, yellow spreader, green windows, 1970, MIMB
**$25**

70 (D) Ferrari 308 GTB, red and gray body, "Ferrari" tampo, 1981, MIMB
**$18**

71 (A) Ford Wreck Truck, red cab and boom, white back, red hook, "Esso" labels, 1970, MIMB **$30**

71 (B) Jumbo Jet Chopper, blue body, chrome engine, 1973, MIMB **$18**

72 (A) Jeep, yellow body, red interior, 1970, MIMB **$25**

72 (C) Bomag, yellow body, red interior, 1979, MIMB **$15**

72 (E) Dodge Commando, red cab, black base, white container, "Pepsi",
1982, MIMB **$15**

73 (B) Weasel, green body, black barrel, 1974, MIMB **$15**

74 (A) Daimler Bus, pink body, "Esso Extra Petrol" labels, 1970, MIMB **$30**

74 (C) Cougar Villager, blue body, yellow interior, 1978, MIMB **$15**

75 (A) Ferrari Berlinetta, red body, 1970, MIMB **$30**

75 (B) Alfa Carabo, red body, yellow and green stripes, 1971, MIMB **$15**

# Post-Lesney Superfast™

1 Dodge Viper GTS, Blue body, white stripes, gray interior, 1997, **$3**

1 Mercedes Benz CLK Convertible, green body, tan interior, 1999, **$3**

1 Whistle Car, gold body, blue fenders, 2004 toy fair design, 2004, **$12**

2 Pontiac Fiero, white and blue body, orange stripe and "85" design, 1985, **$5**

3 Humvee, green and black camo design, green gun, black windows, 1994,
**$3**

3 Alfa Romeo 155, white body, black wing and base, red "Alfa 155, 8" design,
1997, **$3**

4 1997 Chevrolet Corvette, red body, black interior, "Corvette" letter on windshield, 1997, **$3**

5 4 X 4 Jeep with Roll bar, red body, black interior, yellow "Golden Eagle" design on hood, 1982, **$5**

6 Ford Supervan II, white body, black stripes with "Ford Supervan 2" lettering, 1986, **$4**

6 Opel Speedster, silver body, red interior, smoke colored windshield, 2003, **$3**

7 Ford Thunderbird Stock Car, red body, blue and white "Peterson Pistons 17" lettering, 1993, **$3**

7 Ferrari 360 Spider, silver body, black interior, "Hero City™" logo, 2003, **$5**

8 Vauxhall Astra Gte / Opel Kadett GSI with Roof Light, white body, green doors and hood, "Polizei" lettering, 1987, **$5**

8 Airport Fire Truck, orange body, white ladder, blue "Fire 5" lettering, 1992, **$4**

9 AMX Pro Stocker, maroon body, white "Dr. Pepper 4" lettering, 1983, **$7**

9 Toyota MR2, white body, yellow/orange/red stripe, "MR2" "Pace Car" "Toyota" lettering, 1986, **$5**

9 Porsche 911 Turbo, red body, "Hero City™" logo, yellow and black "Porsche 9" lettering, 2003, **$3**

10 Dodge Viper RT 10, yellow body, black interior, "Matchbox™ Forum 1998" lettering, promo, 1994, **$12**

11 IMSA Mustang, black body, white stripes and "Mach 1", green and yellow flames, 1984, **$5**

11 Chrysler Atlantic, gold body, black interior, 1997, **$3**

11 Emergency Response 4 x 4, silver body, red base and back, "Unit 11" cross design, 2003, **$2**

12 Mercedes Benz 500SL, gray body, dark blue interior, 1990, **$4**

13 Ford Open Back Truck, yellow body, red windows, orange and black "24 4 X 4" design, 1982, **$5**

13 The Buster, red body, yellow and white flames, 1996, **$3**

14 1983 Chevrolet Corvette, gray body, red interior, "83 Vette" lettering, 1983, **$5**

14 1987 Chevrolet Corvette red body, black interior, white "Corvette" lettering, 1988, **$3**

15 Saab 9000 Turbo, red body, orange interior, 1988, **$4**

15 Alfa Romeo SZ, white body, red and blue "205" lettering, 1991, **$4**

15 Ford Mustang Mach III, blue body, orange stripe, 1994, **$3**

16 F1 Racer, blue and red body, "Good Year/STP/20" lettering, 1984, **$7**

16 Car Carrier, orange body, gray ramp, blue windows, 2003, **$2**

17 Ford Escort Cabriolet, blue body, gray interior, "XR3i" lettering, 1985, **$4**

17 Ferrari 456 GT, dark red body, tan interior, 1994, **$4**

17 '99 Ford Mustang Coupe, green body, tan interior, 1999, **$3**

19 Trash Truck, yellow body, green dump, "Action Bros." tampo, 2003, **$2**

20 4 X 4 Jeep with Canopy, tan body and top, camo tampo, 1982, **$4**

20 Pontiac Firebird Ram Air, yellow body, black interior and "Formula V8" lettering, 1997, **$4**

21 Chevrolet Breakdown Van, yellow body, red stripes, "Auto Relay" lettering, 1985, **$4**

21 Cadillac Escalade, black body, yellow and white design, 2003, **$2**

22 Ford Mini Pick Up with Canopy, red body, white canopy, "Aspen Ski Holidays" lettering, 1982, **$5**

22 Lamborghini Diablo, blue body, orange interior, orange and white slash design, 1992, **$3**

23 Honda ATC 250R, red body, blue seat, 1985, **$5**

23 Road Roller™, yellow and red body, black rollers, 2003, **$2**

24 Nissan 300 ZX Turbo, gray and black body, gold stripes and "Turbo" lettering, 1986, **$7**

24 Chevy Transport Bus, beige body, blue "Metro Motel Shuttle" lettering, 1999, **$3**

24 Scion XB, silver body, dark gray windows, 2005, **$2**

25 Demolition Machine, blue body, orange hook, black base, 2003, **$2**

26 Volvo Tilt Truck, white body, black stripes, red "Perelli" lettering, 1984, **$6**

26 Police Sport SUV, silver body, blue windows and "Police" lettering, 2003, **$2**

27 Jeep Cherokee, green body, tan base, 1986, **$3**

28 Dodge Daytona Turbo Z, red body, yellow and blue stripes, "Turbo Z" lettering, 1984, **$5**

28 Mitsubishi 3000 GT Spyder, red body, gray interior, 1995, **$4**

30 Mercedes 280 GE, white body, orange stripe, "Mountain" lettering, 1985, **$2**

30 Toyota Supra Turbo, yellow and orange body, "Toy Fair 1996" design, 1995, **$15**

30 Cap'N Cop, white body, blue base and cap, 2004, **$2**

31 Rover Sterling, blue body and tires, My First Matchbox design, 1988, **$5**

31 Jaguar XJ 220, yellow and orange body, blue tire track design, gold wheels, 1993, **$3**

31 1957 Chevrolet Bel Air Hardtop, red body, white interior, 1998, **$5**

31 Volkswagen Beetle Taxi, green body, white top, 2003, **$3**

32 Modified Racer, orange body, "12 Good Year" lettering, 1988, **$4**

32 Nissan Xterra with Kayaks, blue body, red base, "MCH Outfitters" lettering, 2001, **$3**

32 4 X 4 Fire Crusher, burgundy body, "Alarm Unit" lettering, blue windows, 2003, **$2**

33 Renault 11, black body, silver stripes and "turbo" lettering, tan interior, 1986, **$4**

33 Ford Utility Truck, beige body, green buckets, "14 Tree Care" lettering, 1989, **$3**

34 Sprint Racer, red body, chrome wing, "2 Rollin' Thunder" lettering, 1990, **$3**

34 Plymouth Prowler™ Concept Vehicle, purple body, "2002 Matchbox Toy Show" lettering, 1995, **$10**

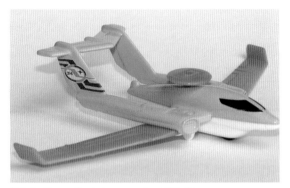

34 Radar Plane, yellow body, orange wings, 2003, **$2**

35 Land Rover Ninety, blue and gray body, red stripe, 1987, **$4**

35 AMG Mercedes C Class, silver body, yellow interior, blue "35 Camsport" design, 1996, **$3**

35 Police Cycle, black body, gray saddlebags, "Police" lettering, 1999, **$3**

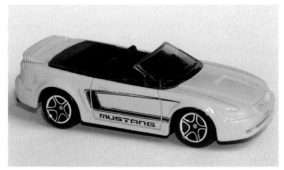

36 '99 Ford Mustang Convertible, yellow body, black interior and "Mustang" lettering, 1999, **$3**

37 Jeep 4 X 4, burgundy body, gray base, black interior, 1984, **$3**

38 Ford Courier, blue body, "Matchbox™ The Ideal Premium" lettering, 1991, **$12**

38 Mercedes 600 SEL, silver and gray body, off white interior, 1992, **$4**

39 BMW 323i Cabriolet, red body, brown interior, "323i" lettering, 1985, **$5**

39 Ford Bronco II, blue body, orange "4 X 4" lettering, 1987, **$3**

41 Jaguar XJ6, burgundy body, tan interior, 1987, **$4**

41 Sea Rescue Helicopter, black body, yellow and red stripes, 2003, **$2**

43 Mercedes 500 SEC, white body, black "AMG" stripe design, 1984, **$4**

43 Lincoln Town Car, burgundy body, chrome base, 1989, **$4**

44 Citroen 15 CV, black body, 1983, **$5**

44 Skoda 130 LR, white body, red wing, blue "Skoda 44" design, 1987, **$4**

44 Ford Probe, dark red body, yellow and orange flames, 1994, **$3**

45 Chevrolet Highway Maintenance Truck, orange body, black dump, "Road Crew" lettering, 1990, **$3**

47 School Bus, orange body, "School District 2" lettering, 1985, **$3**

48 Pontiac Firebird Racer, yellow body, blue base, red interior, "56 Pirelli" lettering, 1993, **$5**

49 (VW) Sand Digger, green body, lady bug design, 1983, **$8**

49 Peugeot Quasar, yellow body, blue tires, My First Matchbox design, 1986, **$5**

49 Volkswagen Concept 1, orange body, black roof, 1996, **$5**

50 4 X 4 Chevy Blazer, white body, orange and yellow "EMS" design, 1984, **$4**

51 Chevrolet Camaro IROC Z-28, green body, yellow and red flames design, 1986, **$7**

51 Ford Ambulance, yellow and red, "Matchbox 27 911" design, 1997, **$3**

52 Isuzu Amigo, blue body, "Isuzu Amigo" lettering, 1991, **$4**

52 Ford Escort RS Cosworth, burgundy body, yellow splash design, 1994, **$3**

53 Ford Flareside Pick Up, orange body, white body, "Baja Bouncer" lettering, 1982, **$4**

53 Ford LTD Taxi, yellow body, "56 XYZ Cab" lettering, 1992, **$3**

53 '62 VW Beetle, blue body, "Beetle" design, 1999, **$5**

53 Police Car, black body, blue base, "Highway Patrol" lettering, Hero City™ logo, **$4**

54 Abrams Main Battle Tank, tan body, camo design, 1995, **$5**

54 Ford Crown Victoria Police, blue body, yellow stripe, "Police" lettering, 1997, **$4**

55 Mercury Sable Wagon, olive green, woodgrain, "Brady Bunch" lettering, 1988, **$4**

56 Isuzu Rodeo, black body, white and red stripe design, 1995, **$3**

56 Billboard Truck, blue body, "Matchbox™ Toy Store" design, 2003, **$2**

57 Carmichael Commando, red body, white "Fire" stripe, black ladder, 1982, **$8**

57 2000 Chevrolet Corvette, green body, yellow flames, "Hero City™" logo, 2001, **$4**

58 Holden Ruff Trek, bold body, red stripes, "Ruff Trek" lettering, 1983, **$5**

58 '39 Chevy Sedan Delivery, orange and yellow body, "3rd Hersheypark Toy Show" design, 1997, **$10**

58 International Armored Car, green body, "MHC Bank" lettering, 2000, **$2**

59 Ford T-bird Turbo Coupe, red body, orange "Turbo Coupe" lettering, 1988,
**$5**

59 Aston Martin DB7, green body, gold wheels, "DB7" stripe design, 1994, **$5**

59 Chrysler Panel Cruiser, white body, "Richie's Burgerama" design, 2001, **$2**

60 Pontiac Firebird Racer, black body, pick base, blue and pink stripes, 1985,
**$3**

61 Nissan 300 ZX, blue body, pink interior, silver bolt design, 1990, **$3**

61 Ice Breaker, red boat, blue base, 2002, **$2**

62 Rolls Royce Silver Cloud, silver body, 1986, **$6**

62 Oldsmobile Aerotech, orange body, gray base, "Aerotech" lettering, 1989, **$3**

62 GMC Terradyne, green body, yellow "X-Treme" design, 2002, **$4**

63 Merryweather Snorkel Fire Engine, red body, gray snorkel, "12th Rescue Squad" lettering, 1982, **$3**

65 Ford F-150 4 X 4, blue body, silver stripe, 1995, **$4**

65 Jeep Grand Cherokee, green body, purple base and boat, "Dora" design, 2000, **$3**

66 Sauber Group "C" Racer, red body, "BASF" design, black wing, 1984, **$7**

66 Opel Calibra, gold body, black wing, 1997, **$5**

66 City Police Car, white body, blue windows and light, blue "Matchbox™ Police" design, 2003, **$2**

67 Lamborghini Countach LP 500 S, red body, white interior and "Countach" lettering, 1985, **$4**

68 Dodge Caravan, black body, burgundy body, silver and gold stripes, 1984, **$4**

68 Mercedes TV News Truck, yellow body, red base, "Matchbox™ Cable TV" design, 1989, **$4**

69 '33 Willys Street Rod, blue body, "313" on roof, white and red flames, 1982, **$5**

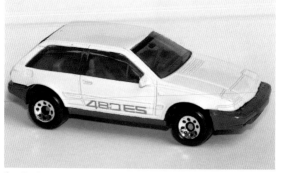

69 Volvo 480 ES, white body, blue "480 ES" lettering, 1988, **$4**

70 '70 Pontiac GTO, blue body, black wing, mummy design, 1996, **$3**

70 Chevrolet SSR, red body, "Ace The Helpful Place" lettering, white stripes, 2002, **$8**

71 Jaguar XK8, green body, beige interior, 1998, **$3**

72 Cadillac Allanté, pink body, white interior, purple and green design, 1987, **$4**

73 Rottwheeler, brown and black body, red gums, 1995, **$3**

73 1955 Chevy Bel Air Hardtop, blue body, white top and "Bel Air" design, 1999, **$3**

74 Ford Mustang GT, orange body, yellow and blue stripes, 1984, **$5**

75 Ferrari Testarossa, blue body, Ferrari logo on hood, 1986, **$4**

# Accessories

The playsets from the 1990s like this service station set can often be found for original retail or less. These will brighten up any display for **$10 or less.**

Matchbox™ seems to have been involved in hundreds of promos like this Aquafresh promo. Look at your boxes of cereal for other offers. Items like these are valued at **$10 or less.**

This set is from the early 1970s. Values are starting to climb. Expect to pay about **$50** for something of this vintage.

Matchbox™ also has been involved in some movie and character promotions. This James Bond set from the *License to Kill* movie is valued between **$50 and $85.**

Look for any early dealer displays. Original displays like this are worth several hundred dollars.

This picture is of the earliest Matchbox™ Garage. This is from the late 1950s and is worth **$200+** without the pumps or models.

Matchbox™ sold other larger trucks in the Major Pack and accessory line that are of the same scale as the regular 1-75 models. These are highly valued at **$100+** in boxed condition.

This is an example of a large early Lesney toy. These were manufactured between 1948 and 1953. Many like this example were shrunk in size to become some of the first Matchbox™ models. These early toys are highly valued. This tractor is worth about **$500 in mint condition.**

The gift sets from the early 1960s are highly prized. Expect to pay between **$500** and **$1000** for a nice MIB set depending on the models inside.

Another example of an early gift set. This set is for the Models of Yesteryear™ line.

The normal 1-75 line of castings was used in a variety of series such as "Premiere," "World Class," "Convoy™," and "Dare." The line was also used as accessory pieces for the King Size line and modified for other series. This VW is from the "DARE" series of police vehicles. I have seen the actual car from my local police department. It is a great likeness. **$5**